The Notebook for the Christian Couple

FROM TWO TO ONE

The Notebook
for the
Christian Couple

The Notebook for the Christian Couple

FROM TWO TO ONE

The Notebook
for the
Christian Couple

**By
Minister Onedia N. Gage**

The Notebook for the Christian Couple

OTHER BOOKS BY ONEDIA N. GAGE, M. ED., MBA

Are You Ready for 9th Grade . . . Again? A Family's Guide to Success
As We Grow Together Daily Devotional for Expectant Couples
As We Grow Together Prayer Journal for Expectant Couples
The Blue Print: Poetry for the Soul
In Her Own Words: The Notebook for the Christian Woman
In Purple Ink: Poetry for the Spirit
Living a Whole Life: Sermons which Prompt, Provoke and Promote Life
Love Letters to God from a Teenage Girl
The Measure of a Woman: The Details of Her Soul
The Notebook: For Me, About Me, By Me
The Notebook for the Christian Teen
On This Journey Daily Devotional for Young People
On This Journey Prayer Journal for Young People
One Day More Than We Deserve Daily Devotional for the Growing Christian
One Day More Than We Deserve Prayer Journal for the Growing Christian
Promises, Promises: A Christian Novel
Tools for These Times: Timely Sermons for Uncertain Times
With An Anointed Voice: The Power of Prayer
Yielded and Submitted: A Woman's Journey for a Life Dedicated to God
Yielded and Submitted: A Woman's Journey for a Life Dedicated to God Prayers and Journal
Yielded and Submitted: A Woman's Journey for a Life Dedicated to God An Intimate Study

The Notebook for the Christian Couple

LIBRARY OF CONGRESS

From Two to One:
The Notebook For the Christian Couple

All Rights Reserved © 2014
Onedia N. Gage

No part of this of book may be reproduced or transmitted in
Any form or by any means, graphic, electronic, or mechanical,
Including photocopying, recording, taping, or by any
Information storage or retrieval system, without the
Permission in writing from the publisher.

Purple Ink, Inc. Press

For Information address:
Purple Ink, Inc
P O Box 41232
Houston, TX 77241
www.purpleink.net
www.onediagage.com

ISBN:

978-1-939119-40-7

Printed in United States

DEDICATION

Hillary and Nehemiah
I am praying for your mates and your marriages

For the couple you are!
For the couple you aspire to be!
For the couple you will become!

The Notebook for the Christian Couple

GOD'S WORDS

Ephesians 4:29-32

[29] Do not let any unwholesome talk come out of your mouths, but only what is helpful for building others up according to their needs, that it may benefit those who listen. [30] And do not grieve the Holy Spirit of God, with whom you were sealed for the day of redemption. [31] Get rid of all bitterness, rage and anger, brawling and slander, along with every form of malice. [32] Be kind and compassionate to one another, forgiving each other, just as in Christ God forgave you.

Ephesians 5:21-33

[21] Submit to one another out of reverence for Christ. [22] Wives, submit yourselves to your own husbands as you do to the Lord. [23] For the husband is the head of the wife as Christ is the head of the church, his body, of which he is the Savior. [24] Now as the church submits to Christ, so also wives should submit to their husbands in everything.

Romans 12:9-21

[9] Love must be sincere. Hate what is evil; cling to what is good. [10] Be devoted to one another in love. Honor one another above yourselves. [11] Never be lacking in zeal, but keep your spiritual fervor, serving the Lord. [12] Be joyful in hope, patient in affliction, faithful in prayer. [13] Share with the Lord's people who are in need. Practice hospitality.

1 Corinthians 13:1-13

[4] Love is patient, love is kind. It does not envy, it does not boast, it is not proud. [5] It does not dishonor others, it is not self-seeking, it is not easily angered, it keeps no record of wrongs. [6] Love does not delight in evil but rejoices with the truth. [7] It always protects, always trusts, always hopes, always perseveres.

John 3:16

[16] For God so loved the world that he gave his one and only Son, that whoever believes in him shall not perish but have eternal life.

The Notebook for the Christian Couple

1 Corinthians 7:1-16

Now for the matters you wrote about: "It is good for a man not to have sexual relations with a woman." [2] But since sexual immorality is occurring, each man should have sexual relations with his own wife, and each woman with her own husband. [3] The husband should fulfill his marital duty to his wife, and likewise the wife to her husband. [4] The wife does not have authority over her own body but yields it to her husband. In the same way, the husband does not have authority over his own body but yields it to his wife. [5] Do not deprive each other except perhaps by mutual consent and for a time, so that you may devote yourselves to prayer. Then come together again so that Satan will not tempt you because of your lack of self-control. [6] I say this as a concession, not as a command. [7] I wish that all of you were as I am. But each of you has your own gift from God; one has this gift, another has that.

[8] Now to the unmarried and the widows I say: It is good for them to stay unmarried, as I do. [9] But if they cannot control themselves, they should marry, for it is better to marry than to burn with passion.

[10] To the married I give this command (not I, but the Lord): A wife must not separate from her husband. [11] But if she does, she must remain unmarried or else be reconciled to her husband. And a husband must not divorce his wife.

[12] To the rest I say this (I, not the Lord): If any brother has a wife who is not a believer and she is willing to live with him, he must not divorce her. [13] And if a woman has a husband who is not a believer and he is willing to live with her, she must not divorce him. [14] For the unbelieving husband has been sanctified through his wife, and the unbelieving wife has been sanctified through her believing husband. Otherwise your children would be unclean, but as it is, they are holy.

[15] But if the unbeliever leaves, let it be so. The brother or the sister is not bound in such circumstances; God has called us to live in peace. [16] How do you know, wife, whether you will save your husband? Or, how do you know, husband, whether you will save your wife?

Dear God,

Oh magnify the Lord with me! Let us exalt His name together.

I pray that You bless each hand that holds this book, these pages, the words. I pray that you keep them focused on You so that their union will be strong because You are the Source. Lord, I pray that their marriage bond last the lifetime that you designed. As they grow closer to You, Lord help them realize that as they grow closer to You that they will grow closer to each other.

Lord God, allow them to bless each other through word and deed. Lord, cause them to be attentive to one another through all situations. Lord, give them Your guidance as they live each day. Lord, help them understand Your will. Your will be done.

Lord, allow them to be peaceful to one another. Peace means that they are cordial as well as understanding, compassionate and kind. Lord, remind them to worship. I pray that as they worship together that they surrender to You as the Head of both of them. Allow this peace to cover each of them. A complete peace which transcends our complete understanding.

Lord, show them how to love each other, the way You share Your love. Lord, help them love the way 1 Corinthians 13:13 MSG, "Love extravagantly." Help him love her sacrificially. Help her respect and honor him as You designed.

God, I ask Your blessings over their marriage and that they are joyful and meaningful. I beg You Father that You help them understand how to forgive—completely and openly.

Lord, thank You for marriages. Thank You for lasting and healthy marriages where everyone's needs are met and all prayer progress is shared. Lord, allow their oneness to inspire others to do the same! Lord, we just want to please You in every manner possible.

I pray for these blessings in Jesus' name.
Amen.

The Notebook for the Christian Couple

Dear Woman:

Your blessings are within and they are exhibited through your activities. As a woman, we need to understand our roles: helper, prayer warrior, and communicator. As a mate, married woman and companion, we have to commit to our role. In order to be effective in our roles, we need to study, meditate, and pray. AT ALL TIMES.

As a mate, there is a possibility of happiness and contentment. In either circumstances, our job is to remain the woman we are called to be, which starts with prayer, meditation, and study.

Our role is to stay focused on God regardless of what is going on or who you would like to blame. This book was developed to help you navigate some of those rough areas and to completely appreciate the joyous times.

The Notebook for Couples offers you a starting place for enhancing you communication, understanding your idiosyncrasies, your mates' needs, and maybe even how to reach common ground. Consider where you started and where you always dreamed you would be. In some cases, those dreams have been forgotten, dismissed and delayed. One thing is true, you have some dreams about this relationship. Whether you have realized them or not, they existed. Now you could have an opportunity to return to them.

I pray your peace. I ask God to bless your relationship and to infuse it with all that He desires. I pray your perseverance and strength to stay the course and listen to God's voice for guidance and direction. I pray that you face resolve, a healthy resolve, so that you can survive your relationship and your relationship can survive you.

I pray that you return to love, that you are able to love extravagantly, and that you are able to forgive. I pray your legacy is built on a testimony which says God is in charge even when we wanted

The Notebook for the Christian Couple

to leave. I pray favor on your lives and that you are able to overcome the obstacles which are designed to test you. Keep the faith. This is just a test.

I look forward to hearing from you. Feel free to share with me as you journey. You can follow me on twitter @onediangage, email onediagage@onediagage.com, facebook.com/onediagageministries, blogtalkradio.com/onediagage, and youtube.com/onediagage.

I can hardly wait!

In His Service!

Onedia N. Gage

Onedia N. Gage
www.onediagage.com

Dear Man,

You are the man! You are the one God holds responsible for everything that happens in the relationship! When they ate the fruit, God call Adam. When Paul teaches us about submission, he states that first you must submit to Christ. In an overall view, we can conclude that if you don't submit to Christ then she will not follow you. If she is not following you, then you are not feeling disrespected. If you are not feeling respected, then she is not being loved.

That is quite a series of events! As a man, you are in control of the temperature of your relationship. Just like with the temperature on the wall in your home, you can adjust with one step. The one step: are you consistently submitted and surrendered to God? Keep in mind that God designed marriage so He has prescribed how He designed marital success.

Man, you are designed to LOVE her. Love is a verb. Verbs are words indicating action! What are you doing? Does your behavior communicate Love? In her perception? You selected your mate. She consented to be your mate. You both agreed to be together. You agreed to be together. You both vowed to work tirelessly to make it work. You agreed to address concerns so that conflict would not start or fester. You both agreed to nurture the other so that your home could be comfortable. LOVE her without excuse, without reserve. Keep your home temperature comfortable so that you want to come home and she wants you there.

Pray for her! Pray for your children! Pray with her! Consistently! Regardless of what your issues are, pray with her. Prayer starts the resolution process. Prayer keeps LOVE active and present.

You are the man! Be the man in your relationship. Take a stand for your relationship. Fight to love her! Keep her first. Consider her needs so that she feels like you care.

The Notebook for the Christian Couple

I don't know what the status is of your relationship so I want to share with you that these questions offer you the HUGE opportunity to reflect on your relationship and identify areas where improvement can occur. Likewise, you will find places to celebrate the greatness of your marriage. Use this time to invest in your marriage at the highest level you ever had. Consider this an investment in your relationship that will have far-reaching results. Your time is an investment. If you give time to this, she will grade this as an investment, equating this to being important to you. If you make this important, then the temperature of your relationship will be more comfortable.

I am praying for you and your marriage/relationship. Be honest. Stay focused. Stay encouraged.

I look forward to hearing from you. Feel free to share with me as you journey. You can follow me on twitter @onediangage, email onediagage@onediagage.com, facebook.com/onediagageministries, blogtalkradio.com/onediagage, and youtube.com/onediagage.

I can hardly wait!

In His Service!

Onedia N. Gage
www.onediagage.com

INSTRUCTIONS FOR USE

Write.
From Two to One: The Notebook for the Christian Couple was developed to provide you with an avenue of expression. It was adapted from the original version, **The Notebook**. As a classroom teacher, I had a student who was experiencing some difficulties with his life. **The Notebook** was created just for him. Upon reflection, I decided that the Christian Couple needed one as well. You should respond to the questions honestly. Feel free to be transparent.

Share.
Share or don't share. Completely your choice. I find that when we write our feelings down, they are easier to share.

Save.
Save your own life. We need to get to a point of understanding ourselves so that we can function in a controlled environment. We want to respond when we have thought carefully and considered wisely the consequences of our actions. This is your marriage—your life! This deserves your attention and investment of time. I consider this top priority, which deserves your attention immediately!

Time.
The time you spend in this notebook is for you. Use it selfishly and wisely!

FROM TWO TO ONE
THE NOTEBOOK FOR THE CHRISTIAN COUPLE

The Notebook for the Christian Couple

GAGE | 20

DREAMED

By Onedia N. Gage

I dreamed of you before you loved me
        Dreamed of your smile
        Dreamed of your voice
        Dreamed of your scent
Awoke restless in anticipation of your presence

I missed you before I knew you
        Missed our walks
        Missed our drives
        Missed our pillow talks
        Missed your hugs
Yet I searched for you

I asked for you a million times
        Asked for your arms
        Asked for your partnership
        Asked for your passion
Make no mistake
I almost fell for several substitutes
More than I want to count
Thinking that they were the answer
Glad I was wrong

I practiced being the 'me' for you
Perfect to meet your needs in just the right way
        Practiced being the mate of your dreams

The Notebook for the Christian Couple

I am prepared to build a marriage overflowing with love
    Prepared to love so passionately
        So strongly
    Prepared for intimate glances across an ever so
        Crowded room reminding you that my
        Love is real
My love for you is everlasting

I dreamed of our lifetime together
I dreamed of our love together

I dreamed of you

When He sent you, I was ready
Ready for our lifetime

Reprinted from <u>The Blue Print: Poetry for the Soul</u>

TABLE OF CONTENTS

Letters	9
Poem: "Dreamed"	21
The Questions	27
Appendix	173
Your Testimony	203
The Names of God	205
Prayer Instructions	207
Prayer Request List/Journal	208
Favorite Scriptures	213
Goals	220
Mission	222
Vision	225
Values	228
Dreams	231
Resources	235
Acknowledgements	237

The Notebook for the Christian Couple

THE QUESTIONS

The Notebook for the Christian Couple

What is God's definition of marriage?
What is your definition of marriage?
How can you align your definition with God's?

The Notebook for the Christian Couple

What is your definition of a wife?
How do you grade yourself as a wife?
How do you grade your wife?
How could you be a better wife?

From Two to One

What is your definition of a husband?
How do you grade yourself as a husband?
How do you grade your husband?
How could you be a better husband?

___

The Notebook for the Christian Couple

How did you arrive at the definition of wife/husband?
Who is that definition for you?
What made you pay attention to her/him in that role?

_____
_____
_____
_____
_____
_____
_____
_____
_____
_____
_____
_____
_____
_____
_____
_____
_____
_____
_____
_____
_____

From Two to One

Do you give your best to your wife/husband all of the time?
Or does she/he get leftovers?

The Notebook for the Christian Couple

How do you treat your wife/husband?
Do you respect your wife/husband?
Do you honor your wife/husband?

How is your marriage?
Is marriage hard for you?

The Notebook for the Christian Couple

What do you want from your marriage?
How did you decide to get married?
Does your marriage encourage others to remain married or to get married?

_____
_____
_____
_____
_____
_____
_____
_____
_____
_____
_____
_____
_____
_____
_____
_____
_____
_____
_____
_____
_____

From Two to One

Why did you get married?
What keeps you married?

The Notebook for the Christian Couple

What happens when you don't want to be married?
What would make that a permanent decision?
Do you regret being married?

_____
_____
_____
_____
_____
_____
_____
_____
_____
_____
_____
_____
_____
_____
_____
_____
_____
_____
_____
_____

From Two to One

How do you resolve conflict in your marriage?
What happens if a stalemate or impasse results after a discussion?

The Notebook for the Christian Couple

What does God say about divorce?
How do you feel about divorce?
Are your parents divorced?
How many of your friends have divorced?
Have you asked for help if had considered divorce?
Have you asked God to heal your broken heart about being divorced?

___

Define Respect.
What is the challenge to respect?

The Notebook for the Christian Couple

Define Love.
What is the challenge to love?

Define Submission.
What is the challenge to Submission?

The Notebook for the Christian Couple

Define Forgiveness.
What is the challenge to forgiveness?

What is the most difficult part of being married?
What is the worst part of your marriage?
Why? Can it be overcome?

The Notebook for the Christian Couple

What is the best part of being married?
What is the best of your marriage?
Why? Have you always felt that way?

_____
_____
_____
_____
_____
_____
_____
_____
_____
_____
_____
_____
_____
_____
_____
_____
_____
_____
_____
_____

From Two to One

Who encourages you in your marriage?
How do they do encourage you?

The Notebook for the Christian Couple

What is the best characteristic about your mate?
Do you compliment your mate?

___

What is the worst characteristic about your mate?
Do you share this information with your mate freely with love, without judgment, in hopes the mate is able to use this information to make progress in this area?

_____
_____
_____
_____
_____
_____
_____
_____
_____
_____
_____
_____
_____
_____
_____
_____
_____
_____
_____
_____

The Notebook for the Christian Couple

The "as-is" of a person: Do you accept your mate as-is?
Or is change expected?

From Two to One

How have you grown or changed since you met your mate?
How have you grown or changed since you married you mate?

_____
_____
_____
_____
_____
_____
_____
_____
_____
_____
_____
_____
_____
_____
_____
_____
_____
_____
_____
_____
_____
_____
_____

The Notebook for the Christian Couple

How has your mate grown or changed since you met your mate?
How has your mate grown or changed since you married you mate?

Does your mate know everything he/she needs to know in order to be in a successful relationship with you?
If not, why are you withholding that information?
When do you intend to share that information?

___
___
___
___
___
___
___
___
___
___
___
___
___
___
___
___
___
___
___

The Notebook for the Christian Couple

Do you listen completely to what your mate is saying before speaking?
Is this hard for you to do consistently? Why?

___

From Two to One

What is the most important aspect of a relationship to you?
What is the most important aspect of a relationship to your mate?

_____
_____
_____
_____
_____
_____
_____
_____
_____
_____
_____
_____
_____
_____
_____
_____
_____
_____
_____
_____

The Notebook for the Christian Couple

Do you feel that you nurture your marriage? How?
Does your mate nurture your marriage? How?

What would you add to or change about your marriage?
Would your mate be open to that addition(s)/change(s)?

_____
_____
_____
_____
_____
_____
_____
_____
_____
_____
_____
_____
_____
_____
_____
_____
_____

The Notebook for the Christian Couple

What are your expectations of your mate/marriage?
Are your expectations realistic of your mate?
Would your mate agree?

_____
_____
_____
_____
_____
_____
_____
_____
_____
_____
_____
_____
_____
_____
_____
_____
_____
_____
_____
_____

What are your mate's expectations of you?
Are your mate's expectations realistic for you?
Why or why not?
How did you discover these expectations?

The Notebook for the Christian Couple

Do you trust your mate?
Does your mate trust you?
Do you keep your mate's secrets?
If not, what happened to make this distrust happen?
How can you restore the trust? Are you willing to work to restore the trust?

_____
_____
_____
_____
_____
_____
_____
_____
_____
_____
_____
_____
_____
_____
_____
_____
_____
_____

Can your mate access your cell phone?
Does she/he have your passwords to important accounts?
If not, why not?
What does this suggest about trust?

The Notebook for the Christian Couple

Do you love your mate?
How do you know that you love your mate?
How does your mate know that you love him/her?

___

Does your mate love you?
How do you know that your mate loves you?
Are you ever concerned that your mate does not love you?

The Notebook for the Christian Couple

Do you tell your mate that you love him/her?
Does your mate tell you that she/he loves you?

From Two to One

Are you friends with your mate?
If yes, how long have you been friends?
If not, why not?
Would you like to be a better/closer friend?
What would that take?

The Notebook for the Christian Couple

Are you on the same team?
What does it mean for you to be on the same team?
Do you feel that you are always in conflict?

_____
_____
_____
_____
_____
_____
_____
_____
_____
_____
_____
_____
_____
_____
_____
_____
_____
_____
_____
_____
_____
_____

Have you considered taking a marriage class at church?
Do you attend marriage conferences at your church or others?
What do you learn?

The Notebook for the Christian Couple

When you are angry, does your mate suffer?
Are you moody? Silent?
Do you ignore your mate when she/he upset you?

From Two to One

How do you handle your anger with others?
How do you handle your anger with your mate?
How does God want us to handle our anger?
What do you do to calm down after being upset?
Who do you talk to about your issue? Mentor? Peer?

The Notebook for the Christian Couple

Do you have 'couple friends'?
Do you have 'single friends'?
Which ones are the best influencers/encouragers?

From Two to One

What do you fear?
What does your mate fear?
What do you do about your fears?

The Notebook for the Christian Couple

How invested are you in your mate's life?
How invested is your mate in your life?
How you know? How do she/he know?
What is the limitation placed on the investment?

Have you considered how God feels about your life?
What does God say about your personal life?
How do you feel about your life?
Why?

The Notebook for the Christian Couple

On a scale of 1-10, how easy are you to get along with?
Would your mate agree?
What could you do to make life easier for your mate relating to you?

_____
_____
_____
_____
_____
_____
_____
_____
_____
_____
_____
_____
_____
_____
_____
_____
_____
_____
_____

From Two to One

Who communicates the most?
Who communicates the best?
How do you communicate?
Text? Talk? Email? Phone apps?

The Notebook for the Christian Couple

How often do you communicate?
Is it enough for you?
Is it enough for your mate?

___

Are you happy to hear from your mate when he/she communicates?
Does your mate sound happy to hear from you when you call?

_____
_____
_____
_____
_____
_____
_____
_____
_____
_____
_____
_____
_____
_____
_____
_____
_____
_____
_____
_____

The Notebook for the Christian Couple

Do you have a family strategy session(s) to plan your life?
What do you plan in these sessions?
Are you participating fully in these sessions?

_____
_____
_____
_____
_____
_____
_____
_____
_____
_____
_____
_____
_____
_____
_____
_____
_____
_____
_____
_____

From Two to One

Do you need processing time after you listen to your mate?
Do you allow/encourage processing time when you present new ideas to your mate?

The Notebook for the Christian Couple

Do you feel that you are heard by your mate?
Do you feel that you are understood by your mate?
Do you make every effort to hear your mate?
Do you feel that you attempt at the absolute highest possible level to understand your mate?

_____
_____
_____
_____
_____
_____
_____
_____
_____
_____
_____
_____
_____
_____
_____
_____
_____
_____

From Two to One

Do you listen when your mate is speaking?
What does it take to keep your mate talking?
How does the silence feel?

The Notebook for the Christian Couple

Define compromise.
What does compromise take in your relationship?
Does it work for your and your mate?
What does it take to reach an agreement?

_____
_____
_____
_____
_____
_____
_____
_____
_____
_____
_____
_____
_____
_____
_____
_____
_____
_____
_____

From Two to One

Write God a love letter.

The Notebook for the Christian Couple

Write a love letter to your mate.
Be sure to affirm your mate.

From Two to One

Write a letter of forgiveness to your mate.
Be sure to forgive yourself.

The Notebook for the Christian Couple

Tell your love story.
How did you meet? How did you fall 'in love'?

Do you lie to your mate?
About what?
Why?

The Notebook for the Christian Couple

Do you pray?
Do you know how to pray?
How did you learn to pray?
Do you feel comfortable praying out loud?

Do you pray together regularly? Daily?
What are you praying for together?

The Notebook for the Christian Couple

Who do you pray for? Who is your mate praying for? Make a list.
What are you praying for? What is your mate praying for? Make a list.
Do you share your prayer lists with your mate?
Does your mate share his/her prayer list with you? Do you ask?

_____
_____
_____
_____
_____
_____
_____
_____
_____
_____
_____
_____
_____
_____
_____
_____
_____

Do you attend church together?
Do you sit together?
Are you same faith (religion)?

The Notebook for the Christian Couple

Do you study together?
Do you share new aspects that you have learned about God?

Do you serve together in ministry?
Do the people at your church know to whom you are married?

The Notebook for the Christian Couple

Do you consider your mate spiritual?
Does your mate consider you a consider a spiritual person?
Do you behave in a manner which aligns with your spiritual beliefs and church attendance?
What can you do to improve your spiritual relationship?

_____
_____
_____
_____
_____
_____
_____
_____
_____
_____
_____
_____
_____
_____
_____
_____
_____
_____

From Two to One

What does God want from both of you as a couple?
What does God want from you individually?

The Notebook for the Christian Couple

What are your spiritual gifts?
How do you use them?
What are your mate's spiritual gifts?
How do your gifts fit together?

___

From Two to One

Do you tithe?
If so, was that an easy decision to obey?
If not, how long did it take to get there?

The Notebook for the Christian Couple

Do you have a hard time obeying God regarding your marriage?
What aspect? Why?
What is your marriage scripture?

_____
_____
_____
_____
_____
_____
_____
_____
_____
_____
_____
_____
_____
_____
_____
_____
_____
_____
_____

Please read the following scripture and comment accordingly:
Romans 12:9-21

The Notebook for the Christian Couple

Please read the following scripture and comment accordingly:
Ephesians 4:26-27

From Two to One

Please read the following scripture and comment accordingly:
Ephesians 5:21-33

The Notebook for the Christian Couple

Please read the following scripture and comment accordingly:
Ephesians 4:29-32

From Two to One

Please read the following scripture and comment accordingly:
1 Corinthians 13:1-13

The Notebook for the Christian Couple

Please read the following scripture and comment accordingly:
1 Corinthians 7:1-16

From Two to One

Please read the following scripture and comment accordingly:
Jeremiah 29:11

The Notebook for the Christian Couple

What burdens you?
Do you share these freely with your mate?
What does Jesus say about your burdens?
Why is it so difficult to give Jesus your burdens?
Why are you holding on to them?

_____
_____
_____
_____
_____
_____
_____
_____
_____
_____
_____
_____
_____
_____
_____
_____
_____

From Two to One

What is your favorite part of sex?
What is your mate's favorite part of sex?

The Notebook for the Christian Couple

Do you have sex often enough?
Do you like sex?
Do you like sex with your mate?
If so, does your mate know?
If not, does your mate know?
What can be done to like sex with your mate?

_____
_____
_____
_____
_____
_____
_____
_____
_____
_____
_____
_____
_____
_____
_____
_____

When you discussed sex at the beginning of your relationship and determined what you and your partner both needed, are you at least maintaining that agreement/understanding?

The Notebook for the Christian Couple

Is the subject of sex is hard to discuss with your mate?
Why? What needs to happen to be more comfortable?

___

What would be the ideal sexual situation
(i.e. number of times each week, being warned earlier in the day, not being told no, you both initiating, etc.)?
Is sex or the lack thereof impacting your relationship?
What are you going to do about it?

The Notebook for the Christian Couple

Are you spontaneous?
Could you be more spontaneous?

Do you need your mate's help to be better at the sexual intimacy?
Have you shared that with your mate?
Was your mate receptive?

The Notebook for the Christian Couple

What could your mate do better to satisfy you?
Have you mentioned these details?
How did your mate respond?

_____
_____
_____
_____
_____
_____
_____
_____
_____
_____
_____
_____
_____
_____
_____
_____
_____
_____
_____

What is your philosophy about sex (i.e. methodology, frequency, spontaneity vs planned, conservative vs. contemporary, etc)?
How aligned is your philosophy to your mate's?
What will it take to close the gap?
Were you aware of the gap when you married?

_____
_____
_____
_____
_____
_____
_____
_____
_____
_____
_____
_____
_____
_____
_____
_____
_____
_____
_____
_____

The Notebook for the Christian Couple

Are you willing to learn to please your mate?
Have you considered a sex therapist?

From Two to One

Is sex better when you are out of town?
Where?
Why?

The Notebook for the Christian Couple

Do you hold hands?
Do you kiss?
Do you touch?

From Two to One

Do you brush up against your mate on purpose?
Does her smile still make you smile?
Does his glance still make you blush?

The Notebook for the Christian Couple

Which one of you is more romantic?
Have you lost some of your romance?
What do you do to keep the romance alive?
What can you do to keep the romance refreshed?

Do you dance?
Do you know how sexy dancing is?
Would you try it if your mate asked you to?

The Notebook for the Christian Couple

Have you ever considered an affair?
Have you had an affair?
Does your mate know?
Why did you have the affair?
Why didn't you have the affair?

_____
_____
_____
_____
_____
_____
_____
_____
_____
_____
_____
_____
_____
_____
_____
_____
_____

From Two to One

Do you hug/hold your mate until he/she lets go first?
When do you feel the closest to your mate?

The Notebook for the Christian Couple

Define intimacy.
How often are you experiencing that?
Do you want more?
How can that be achieved?
What are you prepared to do to reach the goal?

_____
_____
_____
_____
_____
_____
_____
_____
_____
_____
_____
_____
_____
_____
_____
_____
_____
_____
_____
_____

From Two to One

Do you get enough of your mate's time?
Undivided attention?

___

The Notebook for the Christian Couple

How do you spend time together now?
How would you like to spend that time?
Is that going to be difficult to make happen?
What happens when you want more time?

Do you plan date nights for you and your mate?
Do you plan vacations for your and your mate?

The Notebook for the Christian Couple

Do you spend time with other married couples?
Is that helpful to your marriage?

Do you understand the value of time using the perspective of your mate?
What does time mean to your mate?
What does the time you spend together mean to your mate?

The Notebook for the Christian Couple

Is your mate satisfied with the amount and quality of time you spend?

From Two to One

What recreational activities do you have in common?
How often do you get to do those together?
Would you like more?

___

The Notebook for the Christian Couple

What sports would your mate like to play?
Are you going to take lessons or study the sport?
Why or why not?

_____
_____
_____
_____
_____
_____
_____
_____
_____
_____
_____
_____
_____
_____
_____
_____
_____
_____
_____

What is your definition of fun?
Is fun important you?
Is your mate aware?
What is the most fun you have ever had?
Do you and your mate have fun together?
Do you look forward to events/activities with your mate?
Could you have fun with Jesus in the room?
Why or why not?

_____
_____
_____
_____
_____
_____
_____
_____
_____
_____
_____
_____
_____
_____
_____

The Notebook for the Christian Couple

How are the kids educated?
Do you agree on how they are educated?
Would you or your mate want something different?

From Two to One

What are you going to do about adult children when they need money or a residence?

The Notebook for the Christian Couple

Who gives advice to the children?
Do you confer on the advice given to the children?
Do you agree with the advice given to the children?

From Two to One

Who disciplines the children?
Why?
Do you agree on discipline?

The Notebook for the Christian Couple

In the case of blended families, do you include, consult or share with the other parents? How is that working?

___
___
___
___
___
___
___
___
___
___
___
___
___
___
___
___
___
___
___
___

Does your mate change the "rules" after you make a decision?
What happens when you disagree about a child issue?

The Notebook for the Christian Couple

How would a crisis with your child affect your marriage/relationship (i.e. death, illness, incarceration, addictions, etc.)?

___
___
___
___
___
___
___
___
___
___
___
___
___
___
___
___
___
___
___
___
___
___
___

From Two to One

Do you put your children in front of your mate?
How would that make you feel?

The Notebook for the Christian Couple

As the matriarch/patriarch, do you fully understand your role?
Do you fully operate in your role?
Do you seek assistance in your role when trouble or victory is present?

_____
_____
_____
_____
_____
_____
_____
_____
_____
_____
_____
_____
_____
_____
_____
_____
_____
_____
_____
_____

From Two to One

What do you want for your children that you never had?

The Notebook for the Christian Couple

Do you discuss your career with your mate?
When you are seeking advancement or change, do you share this with your mate?

_____
_____
_____
_____
_____
_____
_____
_____
_____
_____
_____
_____
_____
_____
_____
_____
_____
_____
_____
_____

From Two to One

Do you and your mate have a strategy for a career(s) that is functional for your family priorities? Why or why not?

___
___
___
___
___
___
___
___
___
___
___
___
___
___
___
___
___
___
___
___

The Notebook for the Christian Couple

Does your career occupy time that should be allocated for your mate/family?
Does your relationship warrant a change in your time allocation?
Does your travel impact your mate/family?

_____
_____
_____
_____
_____
_____
_____
_____
_____
_____
_____
_____
_____
_____
_____
_____
_____
_____
_____
_____

From Two to One

Does your mate perceive that your career is first/more important than him/her?
Do you bring work home regularly?
How does your mate feel about that?

_____
_____
_____
_____
_____
_____
_____
_____
_____
_____
_____
_____
_____
_____
_____
_____
_____
_____
_____
_____

What is the mission for your family?
What is your vision for your family?
What are the values of your family?
What are the goals for your family?
(There are worksheets in the appendix.)

_____
_____
_____
_____
_____
_____
_____
_____
_____
_____
_____
_____
_____
_____
_____
_____

Are your pursuing the dreams and goals you set forth for yourself?
Do you share those goals and dreams with your mate?
Does your mate support that?

The Notebook for the Christian Couple

Do you and your mate have anything in common in your careers/career path?
Does it help your relationship?
Do you sense any competition between you and your mate regarding career, progress and salary?

_____
_____
_____
_____
_____
_____
_____
_____
_____
_____
_____
_____
_____
_____
_____
_____
_____
_____
_____
_____

From Two to One

How are financial decisions made in your marriage?
How do you determine what the non-consult purchase agreement is?

The Notebook for the Christian Couple

Do you have one bank account? Separate accounts?
Why?
Is that best for your marriage?
Have you considered that separate accounts maybe negatively impacting your marriage?

___
___
___
___
___
___
___
___
___
___
___
___
___
___
___
___
___
___
___
___

When are major decisions made?
When are major purchases made?
Do you agree on these financial parameters?
What happens when these parameters are broken?

The Notebook for the Christian Couple

What are your financial goals?
Does your mate know? Do you agree?
What would your mate like to add?
What would you mate disagree with?

_____
_____
_____
_____
_____
_____
_____
_____
_____
_____
_____
_____
_____
_____
_____
_____
_____

How much stress would be relieved in your marriage if you and your mate agreed on these financial matters?
What one thing could you give up to help reach a goal?
What could your mate give up to reach the goal?

_____
_____
_____
_____
_____
_____
_____
_____
_____
_____
_____
_____
_____
_____
_____
_____
_____
_____
_____
_____

The Notebook for the Christian Couple

Have you had a professional financial check-up within the last six months?
Do you know/understand all of the financial matters in your marriage?

Could your marriage survive bankruptcy, foreclosure, unemployment, or any other mitigation or loss? How long could your savings sustain you if one of you would become unemployed or physically disabled? What kind of insurance do you have in the event of accident or serious illness?

The Notebook for the Christian Couple

Do you and your mate have a secondary, residual source of income?
If so, what is it? Do you work together?
If not, why not? Is there a plan to have one? How soon?

_____
_____
_____
_____
_____
_____
_____
_____
_____
_____
_____
_____
_____
_____
_____
_____
_____
_____
_____
_____

From Two to One

Could you and your mate live off of one income?
What would you have to trim in your budget to do so?
Are you willing to do it?
When would you start?

___
___
___
___
___
___
___
___
___
___
___
___
___
___
___
___
___
___

The Notebook for the Christian Couple

Who manages the credit reports of both of you?

_____
_____
_____
_____
_____
_____
_____
_____
_____
_____
_____
_____
_____
_____
_____
_____
_____
_____
_____
_____

From Two to One

How do you shape your family culture?
How does your family respond?
How did you decide what your goals are for your family?

The Notebook for the Christian Couple

Could you have been picked as Mary?
Could you have been picked as Joseph?
How do you cultivate and encourage greatness in your children right now?

From Two to One

Do you know the story of David?
What are important family values for you?
How did you learn these values?
Are these currently functioning in your home?

___

The Notebook for the Christian Couple

Do you know the story of Job?
What should a family do and be?
What makes someone family?

Tell your Job story.
Job's wife: What should she be doing?
What should Job be doing to educate his wife about what God is doing?
What would you do in her/his situation?

The Notebook for the Christian Couple

Do you know the story of Ruth to David to Jesus?
What is your family legacy?
Consider family education, businesses owned, homeownership, and overall activities.

_____
_____
_____
_____
_____
_____
_____
_____
_____
_____
_____
_____
_____
_____
_____
_____
_____
_____
_____

Do you have a marital role model?
Do you admire their relationship with Christ and their mate?
Why?
How did you select that person as your marital role model?

The Notebook for the Christian Couple

Who is your best friend? Why?
What does God say about friends?
How do you spend your time together?
How did you meet?
How long have you been friends?
What does your friend do/say to improve your marriage?

_____
_____
_____
_____
_____
_____
_____
_____
_____
_____
_____
_____
_____
_____
_____

From Two to One

What has been the best thing that God has ever done to/for you?
Why was this the best thing?

_____
_____
_____
_____
_____
_____
_____
_____
_____
_____
_____
_____
_____
_____
_____
_____
_____
_____
_____

The Notebook for the Christian Couple

What has been the second best thing that God has ever done to/for you?
Why was this the second best thing?

Are you listening and seeking God for your marriage?
What does God say to you about your mate and marriage?

The Notebook for the Christian Couple

What is the worst thing you have ever experienced?
Did you tell Jesus about it? What did Jesus say?
Did you share with your mate? What did he/she say?

Has your mate ever broken your heart?
Did you ask Jesus to heal you from that hurt?
Has the hurt subsided? Are you healed?
How long did it take to heal?
Have you forgiven your mate for that hurt?

The Notebook for the Christian Couple

What does Paul say about love?
Are you 'in love' with your mate?
What does it take to maintain the 'in love' state?
What are you doing if it is missing?

_____
_____
_____
_____
_____
_____
_____
_____
_____
_____
_____
_____
_____
_____
_____
_____
_____

From Two to One

How does God define love?
How do you define love?

The Notebook for the Christian Couple

Who loves you?
Whom do you love?
Is love important to you?
Why?

_____
_____
_____
_____
_____
_____
_____
_____
_____
_____
_____
_____
_____
_____
_____
_____
_____
_____

What is important to God for you?
What is important to you (either material or intangible)?
How far apart is that definition from God's?
What can't you live without?
Why?

The Notebook for the Christian Couple

Why did God make you a parent?
What does God say we are to do as parents?
Are you a good parent?
Could you be a better parent?
When and why is parenting them hard for you?

_____
_____
_____
_____
_____
_____
_____
_____
_____
_____
_____
_____
_____
_____
_____
_____
_____
_____

Do you ever question God's will for and plan for you and your family?

The Notebook for the Christian Couple

What is your favorite scripture(s)?
Did you share these with your mate?
Do you have any in common?

_____
_____
_____
_____
_____
_____
_____
_____
_____
_____
_____
_____
_____
_____
_____
_____
_____
_____
_____
_____
_____
_____

Which Biblical character are you most alike?
Why?
Which Biblical relationship/marriage is yours most alike?

The Notebook for the Christian Couple

What will you say to God when you get to heaven?

From Two to One

What questions do you have of God?

The Notebook for the Christian Couple

How do you feel about your current life?
What would God say about your current life?
Why?
What can you do to make it better?

___
___
___
___
___
___
___
___
___
___
___
___
___
___
___
___
___
___

Define forgiveness from God's definition.
Who have you had to forgive?
Was the forgiveness authentic?
Why?

The Notebook for the Christian Couple

What are the activities in which you indulge in order to escape your issues or pain
(i.e. shopping, sex, drinking, etc.)? Why?
What can you do to stop those activities?
Is this negatively impacting your relationship?

_____
_____
_____
_____
_____
_____
_____
_____
_____
_____
_____
_____
_____
_____
_____
_____
_____
_____

What does God want you to eat?
Could you eat healthier?
What does God say about what we should take into our body?
Is your mate concerned about your health?

The Notebook for the Christian Couple

Are you considered overweight?
What does God say about gluttony?
Why are you overeating?
What can you do to reduce that weight?
Is your weight affecting how you feel about yourself?
Is your weight affecting how your mate feels about you and treats you?

From Two to One

What does God say about how we spend our time?
Describe your best Saturday ever. Past or future.

The Notebook for the Christian Couple

What does God have planned for you?
What will you do for the rest of your life?

_____
_____
_____
_____
_____
_____
_____
_____
_____
_____
_____
_____
_____
_____
_____
_____
_____
_____
_____
_____

From Two to One

Who do you trust?
What do you trust them with?
Why?
What would have to happen to ruin your trust?

___

The Notebook for the Christian Couple

How do you start your day?
How do you end the day?
How much time can you give God daily?
How do you spend time with God throughout the day?
How will you spend time with God?

_____
_____
_____
_____
_____
_____
_____
_____
_____
_____
_____
_____
_____
_____
_____
_____
_____

From Two to One

Do you have quiet or meditative time with God?
How do you define a day as great or not?

The Notebook for the Christian Couple

How will you create a legacy worthy of your gifts?
How will you share that legacy such that your children will have something to work toward?
What will others remember most about you?

How do you measure another person's investment in your life?
How do you invite others into your life?
How do you invest in the lives of others?
What does God say about investing in others?

The Notebook for the Christian Couple

Do you know anyone who is homeless?
Have you and your family ever been homeless?
How do you feel about homelessness?
What does God charge us to do when people are homeless, hungry and otherwise in need?
What do you propose to do about homelessness?

_____
_____
_____
_____
_____
_____
_____
_____
_____
_____
_____
_____
_____
_____
_____
_____
_____
_____
_____
_____

From Two to One

Do you know anyone in foster care?
Do you know anyone who has been adopted?
How do you think they feel about being adopted?
How would you feel about being adopted?
What does God want us to do for those in need?
Would you help by adopting or foster parenting?

_____
_____
_____
_____
_____
_____
_____
_____
_____
_____
_____
_____
_____
_____
_____
_____

The Notebook for the Christian Couple

Have you discussed death with your mate?
Do you have a will? Together?
What are your wishes?

_____
_____
_____
_____
_____
_____
_____
_____
_____
_____
_____
_____
_____
_____
_____
_____
_____
_____
_____
_____

Reflections

The Notebook for the Christian Couple

Reflections

_____
_____
_____
_____
_____
_____
_____
_____
_____
_____
_____
_____
_____
_____
_____
_____
_____
_____
_____
_____

Reflections

The Notebook for the Christian Couple

Reflections

Appendix

Your Testimony	203
The Names of God	205
Prayer Instructions	207
Prayer Request List/Journal	208
Favorite Scriptures	213
Goals	220
Mission	222
Vision	225
Values	228
Dreams	231

The Notebook for the Christian Couple

Your Testimony

Your testimony is your experience with God and the results of that experience. This includes your first encounter with Christ to your current life.

Consider the answers to the following questions to develop your testimony:
1. What has God delivered you from in your marriage?
2. How do you help others with their marriage?
3. What has been the lesson with your marriage?
4. What is your relationship with God like?
5. What danger has He kept you from?
6. What have you done that would have sabotaged God's work if He had not stopped you?
7. What has happened that you realized that only God was in charge to make this happen?

_____
_____
_____
_____
_____
_____
_____
_____
_____
_____
_____
_____
_____
_____
_____

The Notebook for the Christian Couple

The Names of God

(1) **Elohim**: The plural form of *EL*, meaning "strong one." It is used of false gods, but when used of the true God, it is a plural of majesty and intimates the trinity. It is especially used of God's sovereignty, creative work, mighty work for Israel and in relation to His sovereignty (Isa. 54:5; Jer. 32:27; Gen. 1:1; Isa. 45:18; Deut. 5:23; 8:15; Ps. 68:7).

Compounds of *El*:

- *El Shaddai:* "God Almighty." The derivation is uncertain. Some think it stresses God's loving supply and comfort; others His power as the Almighty one standing on a mountain and who corrects and chastens (Gen. 17:1; 28:3; 35:11; Ex. 6:1; Ps. 91:1, 2).
- *El Elyon:* "The Most High God." Stresses God's strength, sovereignty, and supremacy (Gen. 14:19; Ps. 9:2; Dan. 7:18, 22, 25).
- *El Olam:* "The Everlasting God." Emphasizes God's unchangeableness and is connected with His inexhaustibleness (Gen. 16:13).

(2) **Yahweh (YHWH):** Comes from a verb which means "to exist, be." This, plus its usage, shows that this name stresses God as the independent and self-existent God of revelation and redemption (Gen. 4:3; Ex. 6:3 (cf. 3:14); 3:12).

Compounds of *Yahweh:* Strictly speaking, these compounds are designations or titles which reveal additional facts about God's character.

- *Yahweh Jireh (Yireh):* "The Lord will provide." Stresses God's provision for His people (Gen. 22:14).
- *Yahweh Nissi:* "The Lord is my Banner." Stresses that God is our rallying point and our means of victory; the one who fights for His people (Ex. 17:15).
- *Yahweh Shalom:* "The Lord is Peace." Points to the Lord as the means of our peace and rest (Jud. 6:24).
- *Yahweh Sabbaoth:* "The Lord of Hosts." A military figure portraying the Lord as the commander of the armies of heaven (1 Sam. 1:3; 17:45).
- *Yahweh Maccaddeshcem*: "The Lord your Sanctifier." Portrays the Lord as our means of sanctification or as the one who sets believers apart for His purposes (Ex. 31:13).
- *Yahweh Ro'i:* "The Lord my Shepherd." Portrays the Lord as the Shepherd who cares for His people as a shepherd cares for the sheep of his pasture (Ps. 23:1).
- *Yahweh Tsidkenu*: "The Lord our Righteousness." Portrays the Lord as the means of our righteousness (Jer. 23:6).

- **Yahweh Shammah**: "The Lord is there." Portrays the Lord's personal presence in the millennial kingdom (Ezek. 48:35).
- **Yahweh Elohim Israel:** "The Lord, the God of Israel." Identifies Yahweh as the God of Israel in contrast to the false gods of the nations (Jud. 5:3.; Isa. 17:6).

(3) *Adonai:* Like *Elohim*, this too is a plural of majesty. The singular form means "master, owner." Stresses man's relationship to God as his master, authority, and provider (Gen. 18:2; 40:1; 1 Sam. 1:15; Ex. 21:1-6; Josh. 5:14).

(4) ***Theos***: Greek word translated "God." Primary name for God used in the New Testament. Its use teaches: (1) *He is the only true God* (Matt. 23:9; Rom. 3:30); (2) *He is unique* (1 Tim. 1:17; John 17:3; Rev. 15:4; 16:7); (3) *He is transcendent* (Acts 17:24; Heb. 3:4; Rev. 10:6); (4) *He is the Savior* (John 3:16; 1 Tim. 1:1; 2:3; 4:10). This name is used of Christ as God in John 1:1, 18; 20:28; 1 John 5:20; Tit. 2:13; Rom. 9:5; Heb. 1:8; 2 Pet. 1:1.

(5) ***Kurios***: Greek word translated "Lord." Stresses authority and supremacy. While it can mean sir (John 4:11), owner (Luke 19:33), master (Col. 3:22), or even refer to idols (1 Cor. 8:5) or husbands (1 Pet. 3:6), it is used mostly as the equivalent of *Yahweh* of the Old Testament. It too is used of Jesus Christ meaning (1) Rabbi or Sir (Matt. 8:6); (2) God or Deity (John 20:28; Acts 2:36; Rom. 10:9; Phil. 2:11).

(6) ***Despotes***: Greek word translated "Master." Carries the idea of ownership while *kurios* stressed supreme authority (Luke 2:29; Acts 4:24; Rev. 6:10; 2 Pet. 2:1; Jude 4).

(7) ***Father***: A distinctive New Testament revelation is that through faith in Christ, God becomes our personal Father. Father is used of God in the Old Testament only 15 times while it is used of God 245 times in the New Testament. As a name of God, it stresses God's loving care, provision, discipline, and the way we are to address God in prayer (Matt. 7:11; Jam. 1:17; Heb. 12:5-11; John 15:16; 16:23; Eph. 2:18; 3:15; 1 Thess. 3:11).

Source: http://www.agapebiblestudy.com/documents/the%20many%20names%20of%20god.htm

Prayer
A Short How To Guide

The prayers which are most effective follow the following "rules:"

- It is a conversation with God.
- Be Honest with God.
- This is a relationship.
- God is to be praised, worshiped and glorified.
- God likes His word prayed back to Him.
- This is not a list of stuff you want.
- Think of more than yourself when you pray.
- Be authentic with God and yourself.
- Be prepared for people to ask you about your prayer life and faith.
- Do not worry about big words or long sentences.
- Please know that God is not taking revenge on others for you, and vice versa.
- Please prayer in the name of Jesus.
- There is no correct way to pray.

Scriptures on Prayer

Matthew 6:9-14

1 Thessalonians 5:17

Matthew 26:

John 17

The Notebook for the Christian Couple

Prayer Requests
Prayer Journal

1. What are you asking God for?
2. What are you hoping God will do?
3. What are you expecting from God?
4. What has God already done to exceed your expectations?
5. What has God done to get your attention?
6. What has He shown about Himself and you?

_____
_____
_____
_____
_____
_____
_____
_____
_____
_____
_____

From Two to One

The Notebook for the Christian Couple

From Two to One

The Notebook for the Christian Couple

Favorite Scriptures

Numbers 6:24-26

[24] The LORD bless you and keep you;

[25] the LORD make his face shine on you and be gracious to you;

[26] the LORD turn his face toward you and give you peace."

Jeremiah 1:5

[5] "Before I formed you in the womb I knew[a] you, before you were born I set you apart; I appointed you as a prophet to the nations."

Jeremiah 29:11

[11] For I know the plans I have for you," declares the LORD, "plans to prosper you and not to harm you, plans to give you hope and a future.

Psalm 8:1

[1] LORD, our Lord, how excellent is Your name in all the earth!

Psalm 19:14

[14] May these words of my mouth and this meditation of my heart be pleasing in your sight, LORD, my Rock and my Redeemer.

The Notebook for the Christian Couple

Psalm 46:1, 10

[1] God is our refuge and strength, an ever-present help in trouble. [10] "Be still, and know that I am God."

Psalm 119:11

[11] I have hidden your word in my heart that I might not sin against you.

Psalm 139:14

[14] I praise you because I am fearfully and wonderfully made; your works are wonderful, I know that full well.

Proverbs 3:5-6

[5] Trust in the LORD with all your heart and lean not on your own understanding;
[6] in all your ways acknowledge him, and he will make your paths straight.

Proverbs 23:7 (KJV)

[7] For as he thinketh in his heart, so is he: Eat and drink, saith he to thee; but his heart is not with thee.

Habakkuk 2:2

[2] Then the LORD replied: "Write down the revelation and make it plain on tablets so that a herald[a] may run with it.

Matthew 11:28, 30

[28] "Come to me, all you who are weary and heavy-ladened, and I will give you rest.

[30] For my yoke is easy and my burden is light."

Matthew 14:31

[31] Immediately Jesus reached out his hand and caught him. "You of little faith," he said, "why did you doubt?"

Matthew 22:37

[37] Jesus replied: "'Love the Lord your God with all your heart and with all your soul and with all your mind.

Matthew 28:19-20

[19] Therefore go and make disciples of all nations, baptizing them in[a] the name of the Father and of the Son and of the Holy Spirit, [20] and teaching them to obey everything I have commanded you. And surely I am with you always, to the very end of the age."

Luke 9:24

[23] Then he said to them all: "If anyone would come after me, he must deny himself and take up his cross daily and follow me. [24] For whoever wants to save his life will lose it, but whoever loses his life for me will save it.

Luke 23:34

[34] Jesus said, "Father, forgive them, for they do not know what they are doing."[a] And they divided up his clothes by casting lots.

John 1:1-2

[1] In the beginning was the Word, and the Word was with God, and the Word was God. [2] He was with God in the beginning.

The Notebook for the Christian Couple

John 3:16

[16] "For God so loved the world that he gave his one and only Son,[a] that whoever believes in him shall not perish but have eternal life.

John 3:30

[30] He must become greater; I must become less.

John 11:35

[35] Jesus wept.

Romans 8:26

[26] In the same way, the Spirit helps us in our weakness. We do not know what we ought to pray for, but the Spirit himself intercedes for us with groans that words cannot express.

1 Corinthians 10:13

[13] No temptation has seized you except what is common to man. And God is faithful; he will not let you be tempted beyond what you can bear. But when you are tempted, he will also provide a way out so that you can stand up under it.

Galatians 5:22-23

[22] But the fruit of the Spirit is love, joy, peace, patience, kindness, goodness, faithfulness, [23] gentleness and self-control. Against such things there is no law.

Ephesians 3:14-21

¹⁴ For this reason I kneel before the Father, ¹⁵ from whom his whole family[a] in heaven and on earth derives its name. ¹⁶ I pray that out of his glorious riches he may strengthen you with power through his Spirit in your inner being, ¹⁷ so that Christ may dwell in your hearts through faith. And I pray that you, being rooted and established in love, ¹⁸ may have power, together with all the saints, to grasp how wide and long and high and deep is the love of Christ, ¹⁹ and to know this love that surpasses knowledge—that you may be filled to the measure of all the fullness of God. ²⁰ Now unto him who is able to do immeasurably more than all we ask or imagine, according to his power that is at work within us, ²¹ to him be glory in the church and in Christ Jesus throughout all generations, for ever and ever! Amen.

Ephesians 4:26-27

²⁶ "In your anger do not sin"[a]: Do not let the sun go down while you are still angry, ²⁷ and do not give the devil a foothold.

Ephesians 4:32

³² Be kind and compassionate to one another, forgiving each other, just as in Christ God forgave you.

Philippians 4:7

⁷ And the peace of God, which transcends all understanding, will guard your hearts and your minds in Christ Jesus.

Philippians 4:13-17

¹³ I can do everything through him who gives me strength. ¹⁴ Yet it was good of you to share in my troubles. ¹⁵ Moreover, as you Philippians know, in the early days of your acquaintance with the gospel, when I set out from Macedonia, not one church shared with me in the matter of giving and receiving, except you only; ¹⁶ for even when I

was in Thessalonica, you sent me aid again and again when I was in need. [17] Not that I am looking for a gift, but I am looking for what may be credited to your account.

Colossians 3:23

[23] Whatever you do, work at it with all your heart, as working for the Lord, not for men,

1 Thessalonians 5:17

[17] pray continually;

Hebrews 11:6

[6] And without faith it is impossible to please God, because anyone who comes to him must believe that he exists and that he rewards those who earnestly seek him.

Hebrews 13:5b

[5] Keep your lives free from the love of money and be content with what you have, because God has said, "Never will I leave you; never will I forsake you."

James 1:2-5

[2] Consider it pure joy, my brothers, whenever you face trials of many kinds, [3] because you know that the testing of your faith develops perseverance. [4] Perseverance must finish its work so that you may be mature and complete, not lacking anything. [5] If any of you lacks wisdom, he should ask God, who gives generously to all without finding fault, and it will be given to him.

Jude 24

²⁴Now unto him that is able to keep you from falling, and to present you faultless before the presence of his glory with exceeding joy,

Revelation 3:16

¹⁶ So, because you are lukewarm—neither hot nor cold—I am about to spit you out of my mouth.

The Notebook for the Christian Couple

Goals

goal [gohl] *noun*

the result or achievement toward which effort is directed; aim; end.

The questions that you answer when developing goals are as follows:

1. What do I want to accomplish for God, with God, because of God?
2. When do I want to accomplish this by? What does God's timing look like?
3. Who is going to help me and hold me accountable? Who has God sent my way for this matter?
4. What do you do when you do not meet the goals as planned? What will God do in the meantime?
5. Who do you share your successes with? How will God use my achievement to help others?

From Two to One

Goals

Goals	By When	Who

The Notebook for the Christian Couple

Mission Statement

A personal mission statement is based on habit 2 of <u>7 Habits of Highly Effective People</u> called begin with the end in mind. In ones life, the most effective way to begin with the end in mind is to develop a mission statement one that focuses what you want to be in terms of character and what you want to do in reference to contribution of achievements. Writing a mission statement can be the most important activity an individual can take to truly lead ones life.

Victor Hugo once said there is nothing as powerful as an idea whose time has finally come, you may call it a credo, a philosophy, you may call it a purpose statement, it's not as important as to what you call it, no it's how you define your definition. That mission and vision statement is more powerful, more significant, more influential, than the baggage of the past, or even the accumulated noise of the present.

What is a mission statement you ask? Personal mission statements based on correct principles are like a personal constitution, the basis for making major, life-directing decisions, the basis for making daily decisions in the midst of the circumstances and emotions that affect our lives.

Your statement may be a few words or several pages, but it is not a "to do" list. It reflects your uniqueness and must speak to you powerfully about the person you are and the person you are becoming.

Why should you write a personal mission statement?

Numerous experts on leadership and personal development emphasize how vital it is for you to craft your own personal vision for your life. Warren Bennis, Stephen Covey, Peter Senge, and others point out that a powerful vision can help you succeed far beyond where you'd be without one. That vision can propel you and inspire those around you to reach their own dreams.

Q: How do I go about creating my Personal Mission Statement?

A: A Mission Statement is defined as having goals and a deadline. This is opposed to the notion that a Mission Statement is just a bunch of flowery, general phrases like, "I will be the best business person I can be."

What should you include when writing a great personal mission statement?

- describe your best characteristics and how you express them
- have specific, measurable outcomes (or goals)
- have a deadline — for example, December 31st 2012, or a year from today.

When Stephen Covey talks about 'mission statement' in this quote, he is referring to the articulation of your life purpose. "If you don't set your goals based upon your Mission Statement, you may be climbing the ladder of success only to realize, when you get to the top, you're on the WRONG BUILDING." **Stephen Covey – 7 Habits of Highly Effective People.**

Mission Statement Example – Poor (It's more like a Vision Statement)

"I aspire to start my own business. I want to help others and be a better businesswoman. I will deliver the best food with the highest service levels." Jane

Mission Statement Example – Better

"I will start my business within 3 months and plan to grow it to $500,000 in revenues within a year. Using this success, my staff and I will spread the word to local schools and businesses about eco-friendly food production in order that we reach at least 100 people within the same time frame. My purpose will be to massively add value to our local community in measurable ways that have a real impact on people's health now and in the future," Jane.

What to do with your Mission Statement?

So now we have a mission, we can set a range of goals on the road to achieving your outcomes and dreams. Your values are clarified and should be in line with the goals you want to achieve in life so you should find it easier to make decisions and to do the "right thing" because you can simply ask yourself, "Will this help me achieve my mission?"

You can even put your mission statement in an area where your family or even co-workers will see it. For, a mission statement defines who you are and what you stand for. This lets people see how you think and feel, which in turn, will help them respect, think and act in line with your values too.

The Notebook for the Christian Couple

Mission Statement

Vision Statement

A personal vision/mission statement is the framework for creating a powerful life.

Your personal vision statement provides the direction necessary to guide the course of your days and the choices you make about your life.

The idea is to craft a broad based idea about your life and what will really make it exciting and fulfilling, that's your life vision.

From the vision, you craft a more focused and action orientated "mission" statement based on "purpose." And finally you get to a list of goals, wishes, desires and needs.

In his book 'The Success Principles,' Jack Canfield tells us that in order to create a balanced and successful life; your vision needs to include the following seven areas:

1. work and career
2. finances
3. recreation and free time
4. health and fitness
5. relationships
6. personal goals
7. contribution to the larger community

It does not include the distinctive ways that you intend to accomplish your purpose.

Why Write a Personal Vision Statement?

To express:

- your purpose
- your life's dream
- your core values & beliefs
- what you want for yourself

- what you want to contribute to others
- what you want to be

Characteristics of a Vision Statement:

- Engages your heart & spirit
- Taps into embedded concerns & needs
- Asserts what you want to create
- Is something worth going for
- Provides meaning to the work you do
- Is a little cloudy and grand
- Is simple
- Is a living document
- Provides a starting place from which to get more specificity
- Is based on quality and dedication

Key Elements of a Vision Statement:

- Written down and referred to daily
- Written in present tense, as if it has already been completed
- Includes a variety of activities and time frames
- Filled with descriptive details that anchor it to reality

What Visions Are Not:

- A mission statement: "Why do we exist now?"
- A strategic plan: "How do we plan to get there?"
- A set of objectives: "We will accomplish X by Y time to Z% target audience."

Use these questions to guide your thoughts:

- What are the ten things you most enjoy doing? Be honest. These are the ten things without which your weeks, months, and years would feel incomplete.
- What three things must you do every single day to feel fulfilled in your work?
- What are your five-six most important values?

- Your life has a number of important facets or dimensions, all of which deserve some attention in your personal vision statement.
- Write one important goal for each of them: physical, spiritual, work or career, family, social relationships, financial security, mental improvement and attention, and fun.
- If you never had to work another day in your life, how would you spend your time instead of working?
- When your life is ending, what will you regret not doing, seeing, or achieving?
- What strengths have other people commented on about you and your accomplishments? What strengths do you see in yourself?

The Notebook for the Christian Couple

Vision Statement

Values Statement

A personal **value** is absolute or relative and ethical value, the assumption of which can be the basis for ethical action. A *value system* is a set of consistent values and measures. A *principle value* is a foundation upon which other values and measures of integrity are based.

Some values are physiologically determined and are normally considered objective, such as a desire to avoid physical pain or to seek pleasure. Other values are considered subjective, vary across individuals and cultures, and are in many ways aligned with belief and belief systems. Types of values include ethical/moral values, doctrinal/ideological (religious, political) values, social values, and aesthetic values. It is debated whether some values that are not clearly physiologically determined, such as altruism, are intrinsic, and whether some, such as acquisitiveness, should be classified as vices or virtues. Values have been studied in various disciplines: anthropology, behavioral economics, business ethics, corporate governance, moral philosophy, political sciences, social psychology, sociology and theology to name a few.

Values can be defined as broad preference concerning appropriate courses of action or outcomes. As such, values reflect a person's sense of right and wrong or what "ought" to be. "Equal rights for all", "Excellence deserves admiration", and "People should be treated with respect and dignity" are representative of values. Values tend to influence attitudes and behavior.

The Notebook for the Christian Couple

Values Statement

_____
_____
_____
_____
_____
_____
_____
_____
_____
_____
_____
_____
_____
_____
_____
_____
_____
_____
_____

From Two to One

Dreams List

The Notebook for the Christian Couple

From Two to One

The Notebook for the Christian Couple

Resources

www.onediagage.com

As We Grow Together Daily Devotional for Expectant Couples
As We Grow Together Prayer Journal for Expectant Couples
The Blue Print: Poetry for the Soul
In Her Own Words: The Notebook for the Christian Woman
In Purple Ink: Poetry for the Spirit
Living a Whole Life: Sermons which Prompt, Provoke and Promote Life
Love Letters to God from a Teenage Girl
The Measure of a Woman: The Details of Her Soul
The Notebook: For Me, About Me, By Me
The Notebook for the Christian Teen
On This Journey Daily Devotional for Young People
On This Journey Prayer Journal for Young People
One Day More Than We Deserve Daily Devotional for the Growing Christian
One Day More Than We Deserve Prayer Journal for the Growing Christian
Promises, Promises: A Christian Novel
Tools for These Times: Timely Sermons for Uncertain Times
With An Anointed Voice: The Power of Prayer
Yielded and Submitted: A Woman's Journey for a Life Dedicated to God
Yielded and Submitted: A Woman's Journey for a Life Dedicated to God Prayers and Journal
Yielded and Submitted: A Woman's Journey for a Life Dedicated to God An Intimate Study
The Power of a Praying Woman Stormie Omartian
The Power of a Praying Wife Stormie Omartian
The Power of a Praying Husband Stormie Omartian
The Power of a Praying Parent Stormie Omartian
The Power of a Praying Couple Stormie Omartian
Discerning the Voice of God Priscilla Shrirer
Kingdom Man Tony Evans
Kingdom Woman Tony Evans and Crystal Evans Hurst
The Five Love Languages Dr. Gary Chapman
The Seven Principles for Making Marriage Work Nan Silver
Saving Your Marriage Before It Starts Drs. Les and Leslie Parrot

The Notebook for the Christian Couple

The Four Seasons of Marriage Dr. Gary Chapman
Love and Respect Emerson Eggerrichs
The Sex-Starved Marriage: Boosting Your Marriage Libido Michelle Weiner—Davis
The Love Dare Alex Kendrick
The Marriage You Always Wanted Dr. Gary Chapman
Sheet Music: Uncovering the Secrets of Sexual Intimacy in Marriage Kevin Leman
Marriage By The Book Joan Johnson
The Vow (movie)
The Notebook (movie)
Mr. & Mrs. Smith (movie)
Covenant Marriage: Building Communication and Intimacy Dr. Gary Chapman
Uncommon Marriage: Learning About Lasting and Overcoming Life's Obstacles Together Tony Dungy
Uncommon Man Tony Dungy

Acknowledgements

God, thank You for Your plans for me. Thank You for ***From Two to One: The Notebook for the Christian Couple,*** and choosing me to complete Your project. I just want to please You, God. Thank You for continuing to anoint me and to invest in me and my gifts, which keep surprising me. Thank You for loving and forgiving me.

Hillary and Nehemiah, thank you for supporting me and my endeavors. Thank you for loving me, especially when I do nothing without a pen and a clipboard, thank you for enduring my late nights, your ideas, the sounding board, the love and the support. Thank you for celebrating our legacy.

To my editor: Kim Joiner. Thank you for reading, answering the questions, editing those errors, and clarifying those unclear areas. Your time, effort and contribution mean a lot to me.

To my prayer partners and to my accountability partners, thank you for the long talks and the powerful prayers and the encouragement.

To the readers who this will reach and empower and touch and affect, may these words empower you and help you reach some resolve. May you be inspired to achieve your goals and dreams. May you enhance your relationship with God so that your other relationships will also improve. May you enhance your self-esteem through prayer and study. May you have courage and peace. Share love the best you can until you can share love without reservation.

The Notebook for the Christian Couple

From Two to One

About the Inquisitive One

The author believes that questions helps to you grow and creates the appropriate amount of challenge. Do not hesitate to ask to engage at a high level of participation, anticipating God's best for you!
@onediangage (twitter) ♦ onediagage@onediagage.com ♦ facebook.com/onediagageministries
youtube.com/onediagage ♦ blogtalkradio.com/onediagage ♦ ongage (instagram)
www.onediagage.com

The Notebook for the Christian Couple

From Two to One

PREACHER ♦ TEACHER ♦ FACILITATOR
CONFERENCE SPEAKER ♦ PANELIST ♦ WORKSHOP LEADER

To invite Ms. Gage to speak at your church, singles, women, men, and marriage ministries,
Please contact us at: www.onedigage.com
@onediangage (twitter) ♦ onediagage@onediagage.com ♦ facebook.com/onediagageministries
youtube.com/onediagage ♦ blogtalkradio.com/onediagage

The Notebook for the Christian Couple

Publishing

Do you have a book you want to write, but do not know what to do?
Do you have a book you need to publish but do not know how to start?
Would publishing move your career forward?

Let us help

onediagage@purpleink.net ♦ www.purpleink.net

713.705.5530 ♦ 512.715.4243

www.ingramcontent.com/pod-product-compliance
Lightning Source LLC
Chambersburg PA
CBHW081128170426
43197CB00017B/2788